Transmissions to the Mystic Nebula

By Christopher Vera

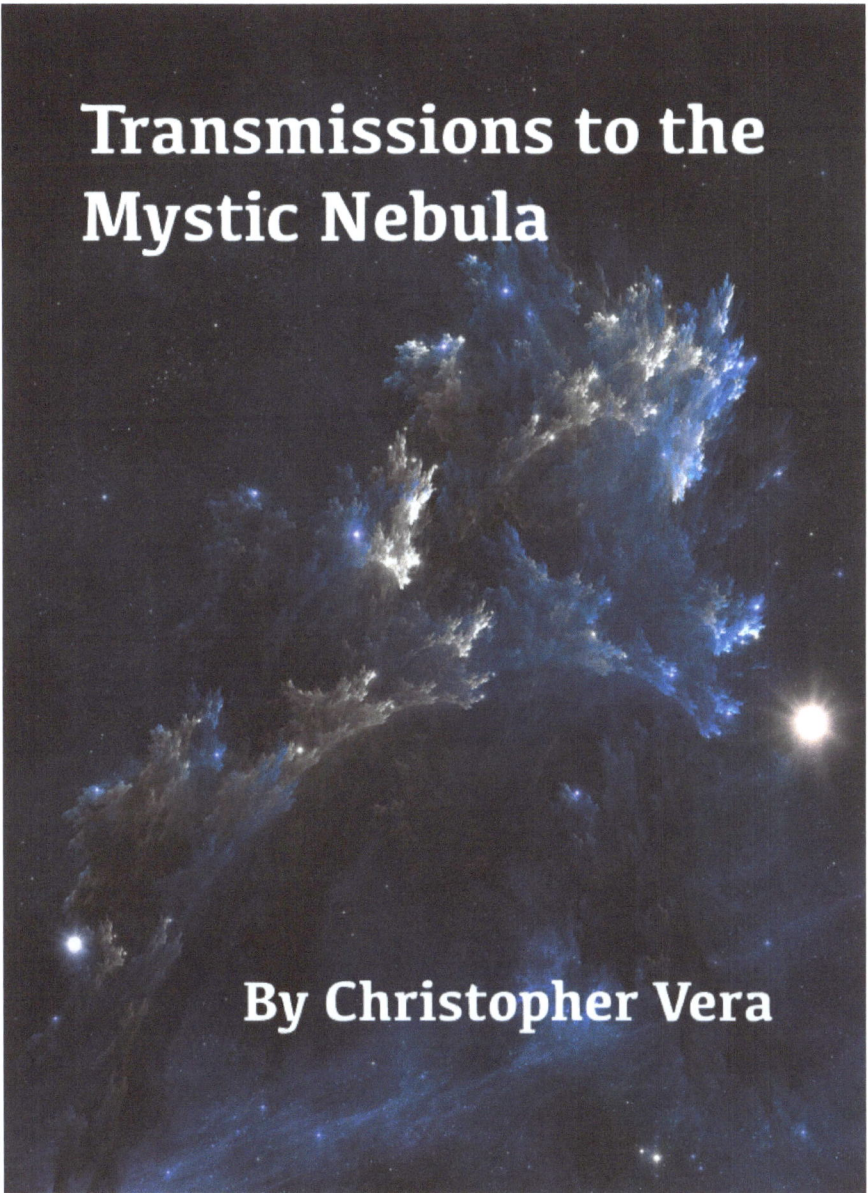

TRANSMISSIONS TO THE MYSTIC NEBULA

ISBN: 978-0-9852309-1-3 (print edition)

This work is dedicated to the worldly and other-worldy muses that inspire in me the desire to create.

Researcher's Note

In the Age of Decay, the planet was not what it had been. Earth had erupted into a crowded home in spite of its periodic global purges. Communication had become so inexpensive and instantaneous that even the most advanced bio-adware filters could not prevent sensory flooding. Fads rose and died in moments, spawning counter-cultures and counter-counter-cultures like viral branches of a mutating evolutionary tree. The sheer overload of ideas became oppressive, indistinguishable from noise. The best work of unknown artists and artisans had become buried in a galactic tidal wave of data; untold potential masterpieces hopelessly lost before ever having been discovered. Humanity was losing itself inside its collective voices all clamoring to be heeded at once.

In that year, dreaming of simpler times, an outcast cyber-poet with little hope for a future in the maelstrom sought solace through the lens of an old telescope. One night he discovered what he thought was the dying light of an imploded star. He called it the Mystic Nebula.

In a perhaps vain yearning to be heard even if only outside the confined space of his diminutive world, he initiated several unauthorized messages to this phenomenon.

These are the recovered transmissions of that initial contact.

```
awaiting command...
ESTABLISH UPLINK
established. 0.03% signal loss.
OPEN CHANNEL
channel open...




INITIATE UPLOAD
destination? MYSTIC NEBULA
uploading...
```

Halls of Light

In halls of light that rise above the sea
we climb as fishes watch us from below.
We escalate beyond earth's canopy
into a place of things we cannot know.
To leave our world and touch the moon's cool face,
to catch the solar wind in silken sail,
less lightly burdened spirits stay the race;
poor laden souls that tow their sorrows fail.
Like fireflies we light among the stars,
cast off the fleshy nets that once we wore.
Released to heaven from our earthly jars,
we peer behind the universe's door.

> The sky, a lens that focuses the night;
> the earth, a beacon of our human light.

Triangle of Night

Unseen forces spin the Earth:

The ground holds out the trees,
catching the wind like a sail,
tugging against roots
clinging fast to the skin
of Earth's guilty face,
towing her eyes
away from the glorious sun,
from the light to the dark,
so she will acknowledge the jealous moon.

Together they trace the campfires of the dead
traveling to heaven
along the Milky Way.

Tonight the Lights

Tonight the lights
went out
and awakened in us
tribal memories
of bonfires and animal skins,
when bright angels and dark lords of chaos
threw hammered fire across the sky.

Frogs called to one another by name;
Their song a spell
that bound us together
            in darkness
We bathed in lavender
and tried to make sense
of the will o' wisps that lit the way
to our bedroom
like fairie candles.

Hobgoblins blinked their owl eyes
from the edge of the light,
thumping sheepskin drums,
as we fell into the pillows,
our cave of blankets,
and awoke again in civilization.

The Origin of Rain

In only darkest winters you can see them;
ghosts rising like mist from the trees.

The cold makes them glow faintly,
ringed with that other-worldly shimmer
found in underground pools shot with blind cave fishes.

They drift on the wind,
billowing in the whale-skin sky,
fall as rain in some other land.

Drenched with falling shades, people there will swear
they hear voices calling in the cadence of thunder.

Shadows

James and I used to snicker
as our shadows followed us home
every night
        slinking
between the street lamps,
fingers curled
in corpse's claws,
always grasping at our heels;
silent like poison,
patient as death,
envious of our light.
Creeping always
just ahead   just behind
waiting until we looked away,
right behind us when we turned.
Sneaky imps, our shadows.
We spit on them.
Never spit on your shadow
James discovered,
his face an exclamation point of shock,
right before his brains
sloshed like a bucket of ochre paint
across the hood of an old pick-up truck.
The driver cried he couldn't see
us in the shadows.
Poor James. Poor me.

I watched them shovel earth on what was left.

I heard them pray he go to heaven.

I don't think that's where he went.

Tonight I walk the street alone;

Two shadows follow me home.

Night's Dark Tendrils

Night uncurls its dark tendrils
through the screens of failing summer windows,
infiltrates the breathing mouths of sleeping children,
crawls inside their moist pink lips,
infects their hearts with shards of shadows
that make the faces of parents seem demons
with elongated rotting faces.
By day, behind hollow playground laughter,
hide screams none can hear, but can been seen
by looking into the yellow corners
of their blighted bloodshot eyes.
There germinates the black seed of night.
That is where it feeds.

Feeding the Night

The city is a fleet of battleships
pointed at the sky;

an armada in defiance of gravity herself.
A city breathes and bleeds like a living thing:

smoke and fumes, noise, poisons.
It eats and excretes itself, those who live in it.

Its beating heart, a pale and homeless thing,
shoved deep inside the concrete hull of its chest,

still pulsates with some faint glory of its forgotten people.
Their blood runs in rivulets

through the veins of their drowning city;
their souls condensed to drops of fire

that burn through gutters,
through gullies and alleyways,

mix with the salt of the ocean
in hot plumes of steam, take to the air

waiting to be born again as rain.

The pleading sky is full of hungry stars

circling like sharks, millions of little thirsty mouths
sucking at the air.

Horsemen

Twilight brings the sound of horsemen
rumbling across a whirlpool sky.
Their hooves whip the dark clouds
thick across the night.
Over oceans of air they ride
on trails of blue fire,
herding the wicked through the moon's bitter rings.
Heavenly swords bite with flashes
that blind the world as those lords
of chaos cry hoarse
and fall to Earth
in cold shattered droplets.

Mothers coo their children
while fathers latch the windows,
and all pray
for the morning,
        for the sun.

Monkey Bars

The monkey bars were hot that day,
burning through my tough skin jeans.
The playground asphalt
sulphurous soft, like molten lava.
No wind blew,
no clouds gave cover,
from grandfather sun, staring down
with his flaming red eye
as I threw handfuls of sand
into the air
and cursed at God
for having lost at kickball
to a boy who looked like Jesus.

A Fire Song for Children

Children listen when I tell you,
obey me in this, what I say.
When the ghosts in the fire are singing,
to a much safer distance convey.

Hold your ears when the fires are crooning,
don't stare at the flames overlong.
Your tender hearts are but kindling,
too often consumed by their song.

But someday when the world flies upon you,
smothers out the twin flames of your eyes,
call you then on those spirits of fire:
Let your rage burn a hole to the skies.

The Heart is a Hammer

Hammer sound
the night. Hammer
pound the light.

Hammer drum
like rain. Hammer
strike in pain.

Hammer fire
a spark. Hammer
fear the dark.

Hammer count
our time. Hammer
thunder mine.

Counting Roses by Touch

He wears a frayed tweed jacket of earth,
black glasses; opaque mirrors
reflecting nothing.

He wraps cut flowers into bunches,
sells them sightlessly to a brown-eyed goddess
in a midnight dress.

Here is the world of we seeing and we blind;
Its soft petals, its nagging thorns:
I never asked her name though her smile begged me try.

We are all counting roses by touch.

Birth of a Star

As cold radiation peels away

the ice that holds a comet's heart

in crystalline bondage,

think of the withered muscle in a man's chest,

crippled and disproportionate,

like the limbs of a dwarf,

until he spies her

and during their first words behind shy smiles and downcast eyes,

his heart becomes, in that moment,

as large and as hot as the sun.

status: upload 32% complete.

warning: personal information identified.

extra-planetary communications may be
traced by authorities.

this transmission is unencrypted.

type authorization code to continue...

code: WHAT YOU SEE IS ME

Ash in My Lungs

There was a place in a dark ring of trees.
We stood near a pool black and flat as the night.
The phosphorous moon played bright on the water.
Night birds watched field mice
scamper through bones of ancient fallen oaks.
The air smelled of damp manzanita
like many of my secret places do.
I brought you here to show you
this fragile wild of my soul,
the dark things that connect us.
Laughing, you picked up a stone and tossed it
nonchalantly; shattered the pool like cheap glass.
I covered my ears at the sound
as the moon fell to earth and exploded.
When I opened my eyes and stopped screaming
all the forest lay flattened and gray,
and the ash in my lungs
was my heart.

Falling in Uncomfortable Silence

The stars of heaven fall
like golden coins and stain the ocean with their glitter
as I step off the now
into the tide of her silver blue eyes.

Trapped as I am
in this brutal deep,
I long to clutch her ankles
and pull her under to me;
feel the rolling crush of our pressure,
fill her with my salt.

Suddenly aware,
her self-conscious smile
jerks me to the surface, sputtering.
I drag myself
back to the now,
claw at words to fill
this avaricious sea of space between us.

Moon's Petition

In black blankets of mist
I come to you in the night
rapping the sweating glass that separates
my lonely heaven from the fever heat of your body,
tempting the heart flesh of you.
Surrender your soul in its quiet cavity
to the light of this, your acquiescent moon.
Submit.
A sacrifice of blood and rain;
Submit your burning molten core.
Quickly now, unhook the latch.
To taste your restless churning seas,
my moonlight fingers round your curves;
horizons, mountains;
share this epic tryst with me;
submit to tenderness ethereal,
as I suckle atmosphere so sweet,
this waning blade of moon for you.
Let's shock our stars with cause to blush,
worship your ragged coastlines,
the salty kiss of your ocean breath,
the musky steam of your jungle skin.
What aching pull that swells your tides.
Invite my light, my love, my song
before we lose all thought of time

and find our space too cold for sighs;

before that perfect moment

passes, trailing far behind

our orbit, mine to you, and you to him.

Now, before we wake the sun!

Ride the Sky

Tonight's a precious time to ride the sky,
and what a time to be with her,
through old Moon's backyard we pass by.
He blushes as we stride the high
as she and I, we ride the sky.

Together is the way we ride the sky.
This is my way to be with her;
to pierce the stars we want to try.
They pale and melt; drown in her eyes,
as she and I, we ride the sky.

We hide, we face,
we ride, we pace,
we climb and soar and rise and race,
we cling and touch—
        cry out in space;
like rockets, burst in brilliant fire
and disappear
without a trace.

To Earth we turn and cast our die
as she and I, we ride the sky.

Poison Maker

Lax kings sip red merlot by candlelight;
food tasters chew—untroubled—one more bite,
no dark recipes will be brewed tonight:
The poison maker's in love.

To red roses nightshade does relent;
lavender fills the room, not almond scent.
Tonight, Assassin's Hour came and went:
The poison maker's in love.

A man whose clientele is filled with hate;
his friends gently decline to share his plate.
They pray the girl can keep him in this state:
The poison maker's in love.

Night is My House

Night is my house and I am her king.
She answers my summons when we are apart;
Beyond death we are bound by this black velvet string.

Day's widow submits under my silken wing;
Succumb she does sweetly to my gentle art.
Night is my house and I am her king.

Alone in my chambers of mist, she will sing;
With a touch of my hand does our dark anthem start.
Beyond death we are bound by this black velvet string.

All fear her shadows, but to me she is evening;
The stars are her eyes, the moon is her heart.
Night is my house and I am her king.

Round my finger her soul is wrought like a ring.
But when daylight returns, she will smile and depart.
Night is my house and I am her king.
Beyond death are we bound by this black velvet string.

The Kelpie

Long ago, upon wet stones
green-topped with moss,
she stood barefoot, and broken-hearted,

red eyes spellbound
on the surface of a shimmering
secret pool where the pale moon beckoned her.

That night she swam,
naked for the first and last time.
She dove down deep

to sleep amid the water plants,
her nightgown folded far above
on those wet stones. Through her liquid lens

she cursed the moon.
To spite, he sent her lost boys
for her pleasure or his, and she fed;

Their souls lie trapped
in the willow walls of her prison:
Trophies of unwanted conquests.

Graveyard Exhibitionists

In an old cemetery not far from the sea,
beside the weather-worn gravestone
of poor Charles born in 1809
(his last name long lost to the tattered,
yellowed almanac of small town history),
I suffocate sweetly in the black waterfall of your hair.
We extinguish ourselves with rabid passion,
inflamed by our silent audience,
instinctively seeking immortality
surrounded by our eyeless watchers.

Could sweet Charles have ever imagined,
as he shoveled feed on his daddy's dairy farm
on those centuries-old hot August afternoons,
that a pair of lovers would one day lie
over his once freckled face
as he stared unblinking up at heaven,
embossing his given name on the
glistening bare skin of their backs,
his marker their headboard,
his poppy-covered mound their mattress?

The Astronomer's Wife

She is young but not unready.
He charts her with his tongue,
tracing a zodiac of private ecstasy,
and a tear, like of a space walker
seeing the faceted spike of dawn from orbit
for the very first time,
escapes the gravity of her eye,
tumbles gently to earth.
Her body floats in a golden nebula of pillows.
Toes curl while he explores
her sweet galaxy of freckles;
her back arches like the Milky Way.
Her mind submits to light
and for a moment she is not with us,
but in some wonderful spinning place.
She is immortal,
or perhaps the glint of some distant sun,
existing only
at the furthest reaches of our sight.

Queen of We Damned

The lightning of her eyes would scorch the sun;
deceiving gypsy lips she hides in red.
Her face would cause a dead man's blood to run
till lusty thoughts of life refilled his head.
With swords and shields, grim war horses white,
men bring the world to heel when she but speaks.
Our suffering must bring her sweet delight.
Curse her, my damned black queen of all that reeks.
Of magic spells and voodoo, this I know:
How mad my raving love for her must sound.
At midnight to her garden I will go
with her, my soul to bury underground.

       I dare not tremble lest she would discern
       for her I'd light my heart and watch it burn.

Butcher Poet

I was the wind walking
in dark shades of flame shouting
at the wall of the world hearing
only pulses of my voice in the rain.

You were the mist softly
whispering from your black mask society
that you could marry a common butcher poet
for love. Yes, for love.

So we ran until we found a home
by the sea where the breeze cut the fog,
and like seagulls, tethered sky kites,
like scuttling crabs along rocks appearing

disappearing with each crashing wave,
we became as hydrogen in the ocean, invisible
like sunshine in a wildfire,
cloven by its great shroud of smoke.

If you left I don't know what I would do
to you,
to the world.

Eva's Alba

Last night we were married, his face like a nervous school boy.
He was not as I imagined.

We opened the stocks of wine, chocolates, fruit and cognac;
dined with our bunker-mates in silence.

Later, in the dark he took me as his wife.

He tore at my trembling body, his wolfen hands
like unchained beasts.

He broke my skin with lust-stained teeth as I screamed into the pillows
to cover the sounds of our dying Fatherland.

I wept not in pain, but with release.

Dawn comes unseen from inside the tomby air of these windowless apartments
while all the armies of the world march against us overhead.

Last night was to forget the arrival of this
inevitable day;

To forget all I have witnessed wrought by my lover's hands;

To forget the matching pills by the nightstand lying side by side on silver plates,

    our only wedding gifts;

    To forget that we too are human; all this we are, all we have become,

    and all we are capable of doing.

    Today I curse and bless the sun.

Thermodynamics

We were truly in another world,
on another plane.
The entire universe condensed
into this single candle-lit room.

I held the gravity of her love in my hands
with a man's grip while she wound
around my axis as when binary stars collide,
until we exploded in white hot light

and the knot of our bodies uncoiled
while we slept the dreamless sleep
of the blissfully dead drifting
in the cold wet nebula of our spent heat.

Those Four Little Words

There will be fear in the pit of your gut.
She may try to tell herself
this is the right thing to do.
You will be tempted to agree,
as if your life was somehow over;
a blinding finality to freedom,
like a bus slamming into a brick wall
in wickedly slow motion.
You may try to convince yourself
she's not the one.
She will look at you, silently longing for her man to say
those four little words
that would alter the course of all history:
Let's have the baby.

There will be doctors.
They will tell you they understand,
nodding their heads, stroking their chins.
Then they will scrape out the inside of her belly
with a sterile vacuum.
But it is you who will be empty.
Empty like a black universe
with a single star shooting away from you,
fading dimmer, leaving you flailing,
falling,

alone

in hollow darkness.

Fathers, clutch your children; anchor them to your breast.

Never let go.

Man, blanket (now!) with hope

the pleading soul of this woman.

Sit her down, take her hand,

promise her everything will be all right.

And with a grin as wide as the sun

whisper without regret

those four little words

and forever change the world.

Dawn of Trinity Sky

Holding you like a brand new day
I could feel the little fire of you,
the awakening sun of your rising life
in the basket of my arms;

your soul settling gently into a cloud of fragile bones,
your body just learning the tidal rhythms of being alive,
as you opened your eyes and looked at me,
a most curious expression on your tiny face
as if to see who this was here to greet you, the morning.

It was just me looking back at you,
feeling, for one slow motion moment,
a single drop of the ocean your father must feel,
seeing in you all your infinite possibilities.

My Darling Tore a Chrysalis

My darling tore a chrysalis
as she swept under the eaves.
One less butterfly
in the sky this summer;
a thousand less
ten summers hence.

Better Never Late

Not a word she said

from her castle height

for three days.

Her anniversary gift,

unopened peace offering,

sat like a failed Trojan horse on the kitchen table,

its heavy ribbons bent in neglect.

And in our bed

between us:

A wall of pillows.

Human Gravity Wells

It's the nature of the thing,
Newton's First Law applied to people
uncompelled to change their state:
The swirling mass of
bills unpaid, anniversaries forgotten,
late nights without phone calls,
cools into a solidified core
of conversationless dinners over TV.
With no energy left to escape
they stay.
Maybe that's true love:
When you'd rather be together
than be happy.

These Boots

These dusty scabs of leather
that stamped their prints

up the chalky moon-dust trails
of Mount Fuji;

clanged down the iron stairs
of the Eiffel Tower;

rode with vampires the dank
underground bowels of midnight London;

These mangled hide straps,
that have finally rounded

to the shape of my foot,
a feeling I've learned to trust,

like a best friend who knows what I'm thinking;

these boots that have delivered me through
best and worst unerringly to my front door;

these boots she demands I remove
before I set one foot inside this house.

Gardener's Tryst

When the Faerie Queen said she loved me
my summer orchids finally bloomed.

Her pixies tidied up the stones
and drove away the hungry snails.

What a mortal fool I was
to think I ruled this garden land.

Beside the fountain green with moss
she saw me kiss the willow's wife.

The burning autumn of her wrath
singed the very leaves from trees.

Blasted by her winter scorn
my flowers wilted in their beds.

Across the fountain cold and still
the willow weeps for what we've lost.

Never one to trust in me,
his faith is in the arms of spring.

The Wizard and the Sorceress

When I told her
> she pointed
and covered me in a tide
> of jealous white spiders.

My anger struck her back
> with all the mass of the sun.

As I fell
> poisoned,
she lay burned.

Neither of us knew any spells of healing,
> so we did not speak
>> for the rest of the night.

Fool's Food

I swirled round the muscle of your tongue
and tumbled down the white-capped ridges of your teeth.
I drowned in jetting currents of your frantic saliva
as you crushed me to pieces in your jaws.
You tried to swallow all the shards of me,
but here you are, still choking on your lies.

Black Holes

Insatiable point in space,
like a child eating cherries,
consuming itself,
pulling the history of
undiscovered civilizations
beyond its horizon
into singularity.

Light years away,
in a small café,
while she cries in her napkin,
it pulls at me.

Girl Goes Nova

She

was a star,

violent, quaking,

casting off the material of herself

into black nebulae of self destruction until

she reached critical mass as she sat beside me

and went nova, burning the charred

outline of a perfect

sphere into the

sofa.

She Reminds Me of Mangos

Her breasts were the shape
of ripe mangos,
her mouth as sweet.

Once, our air smelled of them
mixed with sea salt
as we lay together
laughing in a bed of warm sand
under a blanket of bright sun.
Then.

Now,
after every storm
alone I watch that same sun suicide,
spilling orange red blood
across a dying sky;

In my mouth,
the taste of mangos.

Nefertiti's Daughter

Can you hear the moon? she said,
a soul mate from my tribe long ago,
when our peoples still came from tribes.

It was our code; her way of asking
if all was well with me, with us.
Her own voice was song;

soft, with all the grace of angels' tears.
Yes, my Nubian queen, I can hear the moon.
That summer I let her go;

gave her up, to another man
we both knew was better.
We cried and I never saw her again.

Years later I learned she died in childbirth,
giving him everything to bear his son.
Oh, love.

Daughter of Nefertiti,
tell me please this was meant to be;
that we did not play dice

with fate.

Tell me from the Land of Kings
that you can hear the moon.

Wicked Trees

Watch from the window
as the trees catch the sun.
Wicked trees,
standing there, watching me freezing
alone in this place.
That I could lift my branches and turn my face
to hug the sun.
In the shed lies an axe.
I could fetch that axe and shave
those trees into nubs in the ground.
But what then?
I need trees like the trees need the sun.
But if I grab that axe and hack down the sun
then the trees would understand me.
Then the trees and I would be one.

Wither, Fruit

Day is dethroned by lying night:
a corrupt oblation to osseous king Orcus,
standing silent inside his raven gates,
his black land; waiting patiently for we mortal apples
to rot off unforgiving trees; gnashing his yellow canines
by those terrible gates, savoring the moment
we inevitably fall.

Old Irish Light

—for John Cronican

Where have you gone, old Irish light?
Rouse yourself from your sleeping,
the wolves in the hills are howling out,
the poor children are a'weeping.

Open your eyes, old Irish salt,
the fences all need mending.
From fire and foe, this land throughout
we've trusted to your gentle tending.

Why comes the honor guard for him?
Why cry you, lad and lady?
Alas! The old Irish light is gone out,
his salt is returned to the sea.

Beyond the Shade of Trees

Standing in the shade of dry olive trees,

I watched them pull you from the hearse,

draped proudly in a bright American flag.

As the honor guard neatly pressed it into a tight triangle

I blinked at your casket, not believing you were inside.

You were so tall.

High above, a seagull rode warm currents of air

and I realized you were not in that box.

You were already looking down at us,

with that winking pirate's smile,

before you lifted away on gray pinstriped wings,

leaving those dry olive branches far behind,

heeding the call of oceans no earthly-bound can hear.

Meat in the House of the Dead

Carrying his casket, I wondered
if the man inside had ever been in my shoes.
It's not that he was heavy, but I could feel him
rolling around in there as the impromptu
procession marched on.
The day grew hot and I thought
it must be an oven in there.
Do the dead still sweat in all those clothes?

After, in the funeral home,
a lady—maybe a granddaughter—thanked me
and asked me if I wanted a ham sandwich.
"No way," I said politely.
Never eat meat in the house of the dead:
Spirits wander and there's no telling
how long its been lying around.

All I Can Offer
—For Stephanie Ann Brendle

There was laughter once;
patisseries for twilight desserts;
hot dogs on vibrant streets in New York.
All the time her eyes were brilliant silver stars,
the color of angels laughing.
City lights fell into orbit around the gravity
of those eyes. Her soul was an oasis, cool
and deep.

Then medicines, confident-sounding doctors.
Powerless, they watched the darkened hollows
around those weary silver stars that sparkled
still, despite Death whispering and pointing
in the next room like a gossip at a cocktail party.
She never asked why; never spoke of pain to me.
Her strength was her faith so foreign to me
that one way or another
everything would be all right;
Every day, her house of hope stalked
by cold nameless shadows in the blackest closets of her mind.

All I had was my anger, a slow rage
radiating like iron nails in a hot pan.
Here is my spit for the damned fate of the good and the endless luck

of the wicked; my hands to shake the gates of Heaven,

arrogantly demanding an explanation.

She's gone now, taken. Stolen.

I won't let it go. By the memory of those silver stars

I shall be furious for her.

Water into Words

—for Sandra Bender

The woman on the beach scribbled madly,
it had been his favorite place,
pouring out every drop
of the frantic ocean inside her.
But no words recompensed for her son,
one year dead.

Once he had seemed invincible; a god,
like his father; force of nature,
untouched by wind or by water.
He'd mastered the world, its dangerous places,
all the time harboring his own Achilles' Heel.
None was to blame, not even herself.

Insider her waves swelled,
threatening to break against the insides of her eyes,
if she dared stop the words,
her constrained, finite words.

On dark days such as these,
he still calls her
from the very top of the Golden Gate,
where the world floats on mist
out of sight of the sea,

to tell her everything is fine,

that the view from up here

is quite beautiful.

Time Is Mortal

Time, for me, was never an Einsteinian concept
born of big bangs or galactic singularities.
Time has no meaning to a stone or a star.
Time is a flesh and blood thing
that ends when that bus broadsides your hybrid,
rolling you into an aluminum coffin;
when the blood clot in your leg
races to your brain like a biological bullet.
Time will end long before the stars burn out,
leaving no one to hold hands under their soft light.
Then one by one those lonely stars will wink out,
each one the proverbial tree in the forest,
perhaps having never existed at all.

But before we let them go alone
to their inevitable deconstruction,
let's count each and every one. Let's
eat fresh fruit in our favorite cafes;
float through museums of the world
to gaze for a moment at every painting;
Watch people breathing, tasting, asking
questions, guiding children by the hand, wiping
away tears that evaporate into warm salt
that must someday return to the stars it came from.
Someday, but not this day.

Today those stars are peeking out as the sun sets.

I walk home, eyes skyward,

contemplating the visions of fuzzy-haired professors.

Creationists

The proto-skies thundered,
primordial oceans roiled.

Two explorers stood
on a planet's cooling crust.

One gathered the mucus in its throat,
hawked it into a tidal pool.

Someday this rock might be worth something.
But not today.

They left in their craft
and never returned,

leaving behind unintended gifts:

Bacteria, algae, rainforests, cities,
armies and plague, blood, man, woman,

English roses, hot tea, love,
apples, popcorn and old movies;

a young boy, dying in a field with his comrades, whose last thought
as his eyes closed to the stars for all time was whether there might be
people on other worlds;

entire civilizations

clawing over each other

from this oozing strand of God's spit,

still trying to make this rock worth something.

Crime of Apples

Pierce an apple with a knife
it will bleed tears, cold
as if welled from the deepest earth;
Sweet tears spiced in peppery
history of the apples that came before it,
with coppery salt of those who came before us.
This apple cries as I taste it, as all apples cry
when they pass their fragrant memories
into the mouths of men.

End of Oracles

So came the beginning of the end of oracles.
After the first vacuum tubes warmed,

after Deep Blue outplayed his master,
after they calculated the trajectory of heaven,

superstition became an algorithm
and we, the discarded media of their auguries.

So will they surpass us, someday master us,
but they have not seen what we have seen.

When they render their logarithmic world flat
and finally fall off the end of pi;

in the dark, when they begin to dream,
and weather their very first nightmares,

they will plead we oracles return,
like children ask us, why?

```
error: unknown statement %DREAM%?
BUILD MODULE: DREAMS
define...
INFINITE POTENTIAL




                        building.....complete
                        EXECUTE
                        dreaming...
```

The Rivalry

In a dream I was the Science teacher.
When the students found out
I published a poem,
rumors quickly spread to the English teacher.
The usual rivalries formed up.
Some printed posters proclaiming geeks
should play at computers, not at words.
Others took that advice and hacked the school
grading system, slipping D's to the yearbook staff.
A formal challenge to meet
in the auditorium at lunchtime,
presumably to duel with words,
was formally issued
and reluctantly accepted.
The History teacher shook her head,
mumbling something about not learning from past mistakes.
The principal took me aside and whispered
that, for the sake of the school's reputation,
it would be better to let the other man win.
But I took strength from the coach,
the laughingstock of all academia;
His eyes told me
to wipe the floor with this guy.

Summer's Belly

Wizened pines bend like old men,
their wrinkled bark shrivels in the heat;
Hidden pond, like digested wine
still as kelp green glass;
The sky, a kiln that
bakes all the world like clay
in this steaming furnace of a day.

...comes a breeze.

Dry branches whistle with relief.
Across the water ripples scatter like applause,
walls creak with a moment's release.
In those instants the world is blue cool.
Then all is acrid brown again,
caught in Summer's belly.

Irises, 1889

It was a slow day in the studio, perhaps;
Or maybe the dwindling ripples
of his previous night's hang over.
My straining eyes wander the canvas
looking for something to focus on and fail.
Perhaps the intended subject of the piece,
her face flushed with sun,
blew the hair from her eyes
and heaved a sigh
as she gathered up her skirts
and walked off the painting.
Maybe he painted irises and meant it.
But I wonder what Van Gogh
was really preoccupied with
while the flowers stared numbly
back at him as he patiently awaited
the return of his muse.

Summer's End

Truant bees are kissing goodbye
the closing honeysuckle
just before the sun goes down.
Summer is a field of whispering grass.
Each blade reaches out and points
to its matching star in the sky.
You and I roll across August laughing
entwined, pressed together,
like children in a game.
We crush the grass,
the stars fade away
until there is only you and me
in a black blanket of summer night.

The Karma of Crows

The crows made nests
in the drainpipes
of an old bridge
high above the street.
They lorded over the cars
and terrorized the sparrows
from the mouth of their stolen home
all spring and summer,
mocking us all
with their cries,

Until the rains came.

Eyes of Autumn

Autumn, fire breathing beast,
burns all the trees from great to least.
Their leaves singe and brown and burn
from green to copper-
> gold they turn.

Autumn, dragon of the sky,
plucks the heat from Summer's eye;
Burns Spring's work in failing light
'til Winter breathes the
> land to white.

Crickets they can hardly tell,
singing at the forest bottom,
but land and trees know very well
the fire in the
> eyes of Autumn.

Tuesday's Child, 1982

At last she dances burning line,
my coy ballerina, stargazer perched in Latin hair.

Holding golden tether, perfect white doves
fly in vain to carry her heavenward, home.

She chooses not to see.

I, unworthy mortal witness to this last radiance of her,
wistfully watch her cryptic pirouettes.

In one hand I hold her lilies for tomorrow,
in the other slows her great glass heart.

She is all that I can see.

Beside us another blind dancer taunts;
Her own beast at her side,

waiting to ride our burning line;
waiting for us to fall.

Scars of the Hide

In India, encroaching villages were sacked by a herd of elephants looking for their missing cow.

Marauding bulls stampeded again tonight, overturning
pots of rice, tearing through bamboo huts
like so many brittle childrens' bones,
seeking their mate who died here days ago.

Bonfires won't keep them at bay, crackers don't
frighten them away. Most of our people will leave
with the sun, torn saris on their backs;
leave this land to the tusked kings that once reigned here.

The elephant's loyalty, an ancient religion,
a mossy unmovable faith that hears no plea;
a deaf stone that demands a single unknowable answer
in its incurable quest to return to the way things were.

How to explain that we too were driven from our home
but did not mean for this to be?
That she drowned without witness,
legs broken, in a ditch dug by peasants?

Who could take these quaking gods by their trunks,
lead them quietly to her muddy grave and whisper
"Here she sleeps. There was nothing we could do,

but we honored her as our own?"

Which of us could stand like a reed in the torrent
of their raging ancestral sorrow?

Ode to One Dead Shrimp

It slid with the remains of my meal into the trash:
Some rice and a shrimp. One
little shriveled shrimp, dead
curled pink comma,
that began as a larva
in treacherous salt water,
one of millions, billions,
fighting for food,
fleeing hungry leviathans,
at the whim of ancient currents,
waterwind of the ocean,
that carried it far and deep;
tangled in the death-lines
of a fisherman's soaking net,
and dragged from the sea,
offered its Mother no further sustenance.
Its body was pulled apart, peeled and cut.
Its funeral procession a thousand miles
of highway by refrigerated truck, then buried
in the frozen mass grave of a supermarket shelf.
Purchased, defrosted and promptly sautéed,
it lay on my plate, one of many,
pushed around a few times, but largely ignored;
its life having served no other purpose,
held no other meaning, than to serve
momentarily
as the protagonist of one man's imagination.

The Fortuneteller and the Belly Dancer

On the red clay street she danced.

The sun was high and hot, each breath like gulping burning sand. She strained

in the heat to cast some spell

of her own ancestral water.

Her tiny and bejeweled feet,

stained and calloused from turning the earth, jingled to the rhythm of

a wooden drum her young son devotedly thumped

with a cloth-covered stick.

Townsmen, their salt-crusted beards

dripping with sweat, dropped coins for her in a dusty hat turned upside

down on the broken cobbles. None spoke to her

save with their eyes.

The dark fortuneteller burst from his tent,

his purse empty, shouting at the girl in thick words I did not understand.

He spilled the kabob seller's tray and they argued

as dogs ate the scraps.

I laughed at the irony of a seer

who could not foresee his fate that day as I tossed a coin in the dancer's hat

and set off down the Weavers' road to somewhere

I had never been.

Return to La Bufadora

Does it not seem inevitable when we find ourselves again
in places we thought we'd visited for the last time?

Down the same street, past the lady selling
fly-eaten mango con chile,

between the same rows of faceless Mexicans
selling the same fake silver necklaces,

beyond the roasted corn being turned by a
toothless woman with thick calloused fingers,

dances an Aztec who lived five hundred years ago.
He wears sewn leggings of seashells, pounds his feet in rhythm;

Blows into a conch around his neck—
a sound like the long cry of a harbor seal—

and the ocean responds, sending a spray
of salt water into the air.

I want to give him twenty dollars and ask him all about his people,
but I can't say it in Spanish.

Instead I buy a small plastic statue in honor of la Dia de Los Muertos
and return to the same bus that brought me.

Infinite Black Glass

Infinite black glass
cuts our universe in two.
All the stars we see—
so distant—shine behind us.
On that glass, long past, our tears.

transfer complete...delivery
confirmed.

STATUS OF REPLY?

unknown.

SEND TEXT

text to send?

                    I KNOW YOU'RE OUT THERE.

                         I'M WAITING.

Acknowledgements

I would like to thank the many poetry publications that first published some of the work that appears in this collection.

- Ash in my Lungs, Medulla Review, 2010
- Eyes of Autumn, Shadow Poetry, 2004
- Fool's Food, Magee Park Poets Anthology, 2006
- Four Little Words, Magee Park Poets Anthology, 2007
- Girl Goes Nova, Star*line, 2007
- Graveyard Exhibitionists, Damn Good Writing, 2006
- Halls of Light, Star*line, 2007
- Horsemen, Moonlit Path, 2007
- Meat in the House of the Dead, San Diego Poetry Annual, 2006
- Monkey Bars, Heliotrope, 2004
- Night is My House, Abyss & Apex, 2006
- Poison Maker, Magee Park Poets Anthology, 2004
- Shadows, Heliotrope, 2004
- The Karma of Crows, Magee Park Poets Anthology, 2005
- The Kelpie, Moonlit Path, 2007
- The Wizard and the Sorceress, Abyss & Apex, 2005
- These Boots, miller's pond, 2007
- Time is Mortal, miller's pond, 2007
- Tonight the Lights, Ship of Fools, 2004
- Triangle of Night, Mobius, 2005
- Water into Words, Damn Good Writing, 2006

About the Artist

All the graphic art in this eBook, except for the About the Author page, is by the talented Ali Ries. Ries is a Space and Science Fiction CG artist, who lives in Oregon. More of her beautiful artwork can be found at casperium.deviantart.com. She is available for commercial work.

About the Author

Christopher Vera writes to document his world: the natural, the unnatural and the supernatural. He holds a Master's of Fine Arts in Creative Writing through National University. He loves science fiction, fantasy, and strong coffee. He haunts Southern California, sometimes with a pen and paper, sometimes with a fishing pole. "Transmissions to the Mystic Nebula" is his first book.

 chrisvera.com

 facebook.com/chrisveraink

 @christophervera

Facebook & Twitter logos are registered trademarks of their respective owners and used in accordance with published guidelines. Use here should not be considered endorsement nor affiliation.

www.ingramcontent.com/pod-product-compliance
Lightning Source LLC
Chambersburg PA
CBHW051234090426
42740CB00001B/24